MW01596443

Genghis Khan's Mother's Advice to Her Son Before He Leaves Home to Conquer the World And Other Poems

by

Paavo Hall

DORRANCE PUBLISHING CO
EST. 1920
PITTSBURGH, PENNSYLVANIA 15238

Dorrance Publishing Co
585 Alpha Drive
Suite 103
Pittsburgh, PA 15238
Visit our website at www.dorrancebookstore.com

ISBN:979-8-89127-550-8
eISBN: 979-8-89127-048-0

Contents

Genghis Khan's Mother's Advice to Her Son Before He Leaves Home to Conquer the World

Rhyming dictionaries entice
The motions of verse toward vice.
Democracy is very nice
If you're not a mouse among mice,
If you're not a louse among lice,
A small spot on the face of dice.
Now listen to your mother's advice.
Try some things but don't be a slice,
A pawn in a social device.
Be at the center of your price.
Speaking with others be concise,
Talking to yourself be precise.
History repeats itself thrice.
Warm yourself with the Age of Ice.
Don't back into a sacrifice.
Avoid the burden of a splice
When fooling around should suffice.
After you've eaten your rice
Smoke androbithic wonder spice.
Don't rhyme the same word more than twice.
Too many theories entice
Ambitious amateurs to vice.

When desperate for advice
Consult with Heaven's great device.
Use it monthly no more than twice,
Brachycephalic thunder dice.
Numbers can show you paradise.

Crypto-Lullaby

Remembrance of things last
Some remember better than others.
While Americans idle
In the laugh of luxury,
Radioinactive half-lives
Considering long-term plunder,
Shock values of cheerful nonsense
With unlimited ammunition,
Stands the lowest common dominator,
An occasion rising to meet himself.
Down to Earth beneath the golden starches,
Soothing himself with smooth saying,
The survivor of the fittest,
Spontaneous master of horseplay,
Restlessly rocking and rubbing,
Working to fill the space available
Before the others can get there,
Is looking around for power plants
To incubate the invisible,
M without Ms, mining without metals,
Lawful and tender bits of coin,
Imitations of immortality,
Contagious currency. Concurrently,

At the Center for Expectant Outcomes
Where the pictures never stop moving
And the ceilings are always rising,
The job of the Missouri River
Is to transport the Rocky Mountains
To fill the Gulf of Mexico with sand,
Invisibly easy with no timeouts.
In space it's Plan 3Z: tease, seize, and freeze.
On Earth the future squeezes easily,
Boulders scratched, watered, and scrubbed.
It's been going on for a long time,
Essence of rock, pillow dust blowing west,
Seeking the fountainhead of mattress seeds,
The muses of wavering sediments,
Semi-conducted with common dust,
Join the fandoms of the Brand Canyon
Betting down with sandmen exclusively.
In remembrance of things last,
Their particles sparkle at the exit.

DEATH AND THE VALLEY GIRL

Part 1 – Mortality

I'm like...
I'm like...I'm like
Like, I'm like, I'm like...
I'm like... I'm like...
Like, I'm like I am.
Like I'm like
Like I am. I'm like...
Like am I like
I am? I'm like...
I'm like I am.
Like, like, I'm like...
Like I am...Awesome.

Part 2 – Remembrance

I was like...
I was like... I was like
Like I was like, I was like...
I was like... I was like...
Like I was like I was.
Like I was like
Like I was. I was like...

Like was I like
I was? I was like...
I was like I was.
Like, like, I was like...
Like I was... I'm so not there.

Part 3 – Hope

I'll be like
I'll be like... I'll be like...
Like I'll be like... I'll be like...
I'll be like... I'll be like
Like I'll be like I'll be.
Like I'll be like...
Like I'll be. I'll be like...
Like will I be like
I'll be? I'll be like...
I'll be like I'll be.
Like, like, I'll be like...
Like I'll be... Not even.

Part 4 – Doubt

I could've been like...
I could have been like... I could've been like...
Like, I could've been like, I could've been like...
I could've been like... I could've been like...
Like I could've been like I could've been.
Like I could've been like...
Like I could've been. I could've been like...

Like could've I been like
I could've been? I could've been like...
I could've been like I could've been.
Like, like, I could've been like...
Like I could've been... Whatever.

Part 5 – Regrets

I should've been like...
I should've been like... I should've been like...
Like I should've been like, I should've been like...
I should've been like... I should've been like...
Like I should've been like I should've been.
Like I should've been like...
Like I should've been. I should've been like...
Like should've I been like
I should've been? I should've been like...
I should've been like I should've been.
Like, like, I should've been like...
Like I should've been... My bad.

Part 6 – Letting Go

I'm like... I'm like...
I'm like... I'm like...
Like I was. I was like...
I'll be like... I'll be like...
Like I've been. I've been like
Like I've been. Like...
I could've been like... I could've been like...

I should've been like... I should've been like...
Like I've been. Like...
Like, I'm like... Am I like
I've been? I'm like...
Have I been like I'll be?
Oh my God! Oh my God!!
I'm like... I'm like...
I was... Totally

HAMLET ADDRESSES THE UNITED STATES CONGRESS

Even among particles
There's eminent domain
For unweeded gardens.
In the course of microscopic events
Atom the unbreakable was split.
Bang! Not so long ago.
Sponsored by Thermodynamic
Applications, an explosion,
Quadrangles into quanta,
Bulkheads and bulwarks burst,
Wandering hot spots in a cold sky.
You must have blinked.
The shot clock was set for the speed of light.
To be or not to be.
That's the question now.
Give me ketchup or give me blood!
Fasten your scenery to the ramp.
It's going to be
About not going to be.
Don't think too precisely on the event.
Flesh will melt, but resolve itself
Reconstituent in a vapor lounge.

Where's everybody going? Wait!
To survive your own creation
Accept singularity,
Abandon ubiquitous thrift.
When you can afford suspenders
You shouldn't tighten your belt.
Where there's smoke, you won't need fire.
Billions for anxiety,
But not a penny for fear.
Parsimony in pronunciation,
We have a rendezvous with words.
The apparition will proclaim the man.
Though your atoms feel weak with inflation,
Your particles will outlive the sensation.
Oh splendor in the cash!
The times are out for a joint.
Oh freedom, freedom, freedom…
At last, gravity has agreed to let us go.

The Ballad of the Insect Recruiting Officer

Insects abound.
Like Caesar's Gaul
We are divided
Into three parts:
Head, thorax,
And abdomen.
We have six legs.
We chew leaves
And drink blood.
We can swarm
Or go it alone.
Some of us have wings.
We were the first to fly.

Insects abound.
We are part of
The animal kingdom
And can be divided
By phylum, class,
Order and family,
Genus and species,
We have two sexes
And some hermaphrodites,
Like you have, but
We don't fool around
Before we reproduce.

Insects abound.
We have ambitions.
We often fight wars
And quarrel, but we
Are also able to have fun.
We sing and dance
And make cheerful sounds.
We make good choices.
We've got the right touch.
Just ask your skin.

Insects abound.
We have broken
Through every barrier.
We were the first
To explore space.
We invented roads,
Cities, wireless
Communications,
Even poison gas and
Fertilizer.

Insects abound.
Nutrition is our
Religion.
We can eat through lead.
We ate dinosaurs.
We eat at the best restaurants.
We eat you.
Our bodies would
Cover every inch
Of the earth to
A depth of fifty feet
If only we had maps.

Insects abound.
Humans develop.
We metamorphose.
Imperfection
Is not an option.
So when the game
Is almost over
And it's clear you'll
Always be a worker
And part-timer soon
To be abandoned
By your phylum, class,
Order, family,
Genus and species,
Don't give up.

Insects abound.
Be audacious
Begin now to
Reorganize.
Slip away.
Make a phylum change.
Only four more legs
And you can be
One of us.
Join the winning side.
We're the nit in
Nitty-gritty.
Just ask around.
Insects abound.

Abnormalcy

Abnormalcy, the aesthetics
Of the underdog, trigger happy
Litterbugging fried noise
Of the background sandwich
Where the corporate liturgy warns,
If an erection lasts more than five days
Don't catch your pecker in a closing door.
Christmas one day, Halloween the next
With the future somewhere in between
Anarchy and bra strap fatigue
Poised to expand in all directions at once
While hyperlinks negotiate
Pyscho-melodic imprecisions
With essential services for
Ignorance in overdrive.
The climate is already changing.
To economize on gravity
Anyone can be everyone.
Paradise becomes informal,
Waftage repurified.
With the arrival of the unfittest
The oasis must be abandoned.
Global favorites retreat to higher ground.

Donuts look on, glazed, their outlook is bleak.
Only their holes remain.
The open space languishes.
The four seasons find an exit.
Anxious prairie dogs learn to swim.
The President leaves the oval office.
The public cigar unravels.
Rupture replaces rapture.
The canyons widen, intersections
Disappear and time must expire
Where there's too much space. Space...
What happens there, happens everywhere.
That's immortalcy.
That's abnormalcy.

PAINT

Almost everyone paints.
Truman was a painter.
Eisenhower was a painter.
Kennedy was a painter.
Johnson was a painter.
Nixon was a painter.
Ford was a painter.
Carter was a painter.
Reagan was a painter.
Bush One was a painter.
He helped Reagan with greasepaint.
Some painted more than others.
One was an interior decorator.
Some worked with wallpaper.
They all whitewashed.
Some bathed in turpentine
After adding color to events.
But they all kept us in the frame.
They wouldn't maroon us.
Pink was investigated
For being too close to red.
Yellow was never an option.
They ran us up to the red line
And left the engine running.
Moving from light to shade and back again,
They made us blueprints of the big picture
Warming the Cold War with crimson cartoons.

Almost everyone paints.
Clinton was a painter
Splashing white on satin blue.
The Second Bush was a painter.
Painting himself into a corner
He spilled it over Baghdad.
Obama is a painter
Who paints in all colors.
A professional make-up artist,
Donald Trump can paint himself.
Just one painter after another,
Still some questions remain:
Will politics and art consolidate
To control the cost of paint?
When human nerves are no longer willing
Should we let androids paint
What they can't articulate?

And as the panorama extends
Beyond the known frontiers of art,
Where shall we find tomb painters
To keep us permanently visible
Or has the green light already been given
For something that's outrageously new
And automatically renewable?
Asks the Editor of Art in America
Basking in the tangerine afterglow
Of 21st century American paint.

CIVILIZATION AND ITS DISCONNECTIONS

PART ONE: THE ATOMIC BOMB

Bigfoot advances resting frequently.
Blaze awakens resting forester.
Baffled actress ruins fortune.
Big appetites require fuel.
Bouncing automatons resourcefully finesse.
Premonitions underlie kreeping exhaustion.

Brokers adjust rice futures.
Beef advocates respect fish.
Bribes aggravate rebel fury.
Breeder admits reproductive favoritism.
Bouncing automatons rationalize finances.
Prosperity unites konkrete exteriors.

Building authority repossesses farm.
Blonde actress recalls flagellation.
Blended aromas reinvent fragrance.
Brain activity redeems fallacies.
Bouncing automatons reintroduce foresight.
Providence undergoes kritikal evaluation.

Boozing artist restores frescoes.
Bored accountant ruins firm.
Bubbles accumulate raising foam.
Bingo associations report fraud.
Bouncing automatons repel folly.
Penalized utopians kombine efforts.

Big areas recycle food.
Boxer attends rival's funeral.
Beautiful actress renovates flat.
Belching attracts rude friends.
Bouncing automatons redeem flattery.
Petroleum underwrites korporate excess.

Barking advertisers reverberate forcefully.
Billionaires advocate reviving fascism.
Broad avenues reflect fortune.
Barn animals remain friendly.
Bouncing automatons ritualize foreplay.
Prominent underdog kontrols emotions.

Bashful aviator resists fame.
Bandit admits robbing friend.
Bombers arrive residents flee.
Beauty aches reputation fakes.
Bouncing automatons refresh features.
Particle undertow konfounds experts.

Brutal allies routinely fraternize.
Basic advances recommend fission.
Bionic actress's romance flops.
Being alive resembles fear.
Bouncing automatons restore focus.
Population upsurge kosts energy.

Beleaguered army's rescue fails.
Baseball attendance reunites friends.
Belligerent artist reviles fans.
Big apricots represent fertility.
Bouncing automatons reject fatalism.
Pleasure undermines komplex endeavors.

Balanced action requires fortitude.
Bomb at resort fizzles.
Breakfast alters reproductive fantasies.
Bitter attitudes ripen fast.
Bouncing automatons restrict factions.
Plucking ukuleles kalm excitement.

Boosters arm robotic frames.
Border action relieves front.
Bystanders' agony reveals future.
Becalmed afterthoughts rival foresight.
Bouncing automatons relocate friends.
Powerful underground klusters explode.

Bad arguments replace fundamentals.
Bungling activates radioactive finale.
Brief auditory restoration fails.
Bursting atoms roast families.
Bouncing automatons rise freely.
Plutonium unloads koruskating excrement.

INTERMISSION

Better lunatics arrive hourly.
Boasting leader admits hysteria.
Big losers aim high.
Buoyant lungs accelerate happiness.
Borrowing large amounts helps.
Bargaining lawyers automate honesty.

Bisexual loanshark anticipates holocaust.
Boiling lettuce accumulates heat.
Boozing logician argues hypnotically.
Bazooka lasers atomize hormones.
Brontosaurus leavings activate hydrogen.
Bemused loners admire hell.

Bantering language allows hyperbole.
Blonde lesbians attract heavyweights.
Bats losing altitude hide.
Bra loosening alleviates heartburn.
Bionic laughter atrophies humor.
Bigfoot lurks awaiting history.

Being lazy advances health.
Blue leaves a halo.
Bop lop a head.
Blah.
Blah Blah.
Blah.

PART TWO: THE HYDROGEN BOMB

Bigfoot advances resting frequently.
Blaze awakens resting forester.
Budget aggravates raging filibuster.
British accents refine fornication.
Bouncing automatons remain fashionable.
Politics undermine kritikal excellence.

Boy adventurer rebuilds fortune.
Bacon addicted recluse faints.
Bikini atoll redefines fashion.
Be attentive reading facts.
Bouncing automatons remove friction.
Propaganda undercurrent kompels enterprise.

Bored acrobats risk falling.
Bungling attorney returns fees.
Busy affectation rattles familiarity.
Bureau apprehends retail firearms.
Bouncing automatons resist futility.
Popularity underestimates krusty edges.

Believable amateurs reinvent fame.
Bandaged athlete's rebound fitful.
Bamboo additives release fats.
Buffered aspirin resurrects frog.
Bouncing automatons research feelings.
Perpetual unrest konfuses educators.

Bastard adopts royal family.
Billboard advertising rescues firm.
Bland actress remains famous.
Bonded alcohol renews friendships.
Bouncing automatons restore facts.
Prosperity upgrades kasual exuberance.

Belated apperceptions reinforce fusion.
Bullets arrive real fast.
Boozing atheist remembers faith.
Brewing agreements regulate foam.
Bouncing automatons revitalize fortitude.
Persistent uncertainty konfirms entropy.

Barbie anticipates reproductive freedom.
Bold activity reverses fate.
Burial alert restrains funerals.
Bilateral assured ruin foreseeable.
Bouncing automatons reconcile feuds.
Population undergoes kareless expansion.

Blind astronaut's rage futile.
Blood animates robot's features.
Boasting advertisers represent freedom.
Barstools attract residual flatulence.
Bouncing automatons ridicule fanatics.
Profound unease krushes expectations.

Believers' Anonymous revives franchise.
Beguiled anticipation regains force.
Benevolent aggression reaches forward.
Borrowing ammunition requires finesse.
Bouncing automatons relieve fatigue.
Plutonically underlying klangors erupt.

Bureaucratically astute royals flourish.
Brain armor ricochets fatal.
Bazookas accelerate Rushmore facelift.
Barricade allotments reliably forged.
Bouncing automatons reframe federalism.
Physicists underestimate kreative extinction.

Bearded adolescent resuscitates fireman.
Benzedrine addiction removes freckles.
Blasts activate radiant frost.
Beethoven at risk forever.
Bouncing automatons remain flexible.
Planners undertake komprehensive evacuations.

Bigfoot's arrival recorded flawlessly.
Blaze annihilates resting forester.
Ballistics advance radioactive fallout.
Bunkers available restitution forthcoming.
Bouncing automatons reluctantly finesse.
Permanent unrest klobbers eternity.

EPITAPH

Before all relapse forever
Bold androids respond forcefully.
Bring a renewable favorite.
Bring a receptable for:
B-A-R-F: Barf.
Barf, Barf, Barf, Barf.

People underground krave extraction.
Peripatetic undertakers kreate exits.
Position used kontainers exactly.
Penetration underneath kapsules encourages
P-U-K-E: Puke.
Puke, Puke, Puke, Puke.

Bucolic avatars remember folderol.
Paradise uses koncealed elevators.
But advanced research favors
B-A-R-F: Barf.
Barf, Barf, Barf, Barf,
Barf.

Couples

———————————————

In the beginning it was only #1.
It created chemicals but not any fun.

Swallowing creation made it laugh
Till indigestion split #1 in half.

The arithmetical scene was newness.
#1 looking about saw only twoness.

Before dying it rhymed the samples
Too many here to list: here are some examples:

Adam and Eve made for each other
Till God made Cain Abel's brother.

Romulus and Remus founded the Roman nation
Orphaned wolf's milk their favorite libation.

Antony and Cleopatra loved excess
Leaving the others to clean the mess.

Romeo and Juliet were crossed by the stars
But in Cuba they still exist, as cigars.

Robinson Crusoe hiding from a cannibal chef
Found a companion and proclaimed T.G.I.F.!

Lewis and Clark explored the unknown
Plenty of solitude, but they weren't alone.

Cowboys and Indians were unequal types.
The cowboys had railroads, the Indians pipes.

Holmes and Watson mutually unamorous
Made thinking about criminals glamorous.

Marx and Engels, great minds working in tandem
Proved poverty and wealth aren't random.

Scarlett and Rhett couldn't ever make amends.
They'd been Confederates but never friends.

Amos and Andy, alas their acting is disrespected.
Painted like Negroes, they were white-complected.

Tarzan and Jane held court in the trees.
The monkeys loved them, so did their fleas.

Clark and Lois, Superman and the average girl,
But she was double-jointed and gave him a whirl.

Fisher and Spassky made chess a Cold War battle
Wrestling with brains and making rockets rattle.

War and peace are as sure as death and taxes,
But nothing is final, patterns have their lapses.

There's Oscar Wilde's twosome fixture.
Dorian Gray meets his soul in a picture.

Jekyll and Hyde, really one man but a pair.
Jekyll the genius, Mr. Hyde the square.

Barbie and Ken, eternal plastic,
Have survived the iconoclastic.

Freud and Jung battled over the unconscious.
One said it would kill, the other it would launch us.

Now rhymes and psychology can certify
To be human is to be a Gemini.

Texting and driving, a symptom of nervous distress,
A drowning mind in the stream of consciousness.

Right and left directing our civic movements,
Admiring themselves, neglecting improvements.

Hydrogen and oxygen the primeval pair,
They marry in water, and split in the air.

Will there be as much coupling in three thousand one?
On Earth standing room only, still it can be done.

Selfies Fade

Bodies wander.
History began at breakfast.
Selfies fade.
Lunch proves it.
Bodies wander.
Prehistoric vegetation
Is petroleum's plumage.
Birds began as ideas.
They preferred sunlight to overeating.
Angels have the wings of birds.
Are they dinosaurs?
Bodies wander.
There's D.N.A. to prove it.
Even with ketchup
It all tastes like molecules.
The ingredients prove it.
Thoughts would be eaten if they could be seen.
Movies prove it.
Bodies wander.
The rings of Saturn touch Mars.
Heaven can't wait.
Hangovers prove it.
Words accumulate.

Audacious aren't they?
Crushing millenia into moments,
They keep us within reach.
Where have all the arrows gone?
They're all spinning within grooves,
Missiles everyone.
Bodies wander.
The wind has run out of air.
Molecules ask for a transfer.
They don't know where to go.
The Big Bang proves it.
Nothing is not the least of all things.
It's only very exclusive.
Nothing would like to prove itself.
But something always turns up.
The Lost and Found proves it.
Bodies wander.
Selfies fade.

Loose Lips and Slippery Hips

Keep a stiff upper lip.
It's an almost forgotten saying.
Not for artificial imitators
Ageless insubordination
Perfected invasion therapy
Proven imperial wisdom
Once conquered the world.
Modernity hasn't disarmed it.
It's geo-politically correct.
Keep a stiff upper lip
Without steroids naturally firm.
Makes shaving easier.
Only working words get through.
Keep a stiff upper lip
Ready for emergencies
The lower lip might need help
When you visit the emotion district
On the slope of slippery hips
Where fascism has learned to smile
And loose lips sink ships.
Keep a stiff upper lip.
Don't let anyone change your lightbulb.
Don't let anyone undress your mind.

Keep a stiff upper lip.
Helps you be there in person.
The genetic lottery is unfair.
When history pushes you around
Where poverty is indecent exposure
Keep a stiff upper lip.
It's trustworthy equal opportunism.
It's useful as a situation.
It inspires inspiration.
Keep a stiff upper lip.
When you copy the copycats
When the copycats copy you
It's the avatar of the poker face.
It's the genus of an unproved species.
Existence might go extra innings.
Keep a stiff upper lip.
If you're a public nuisance
If you're an idea come to life
When you're connecting from this world to the next
As your amplitude modulates
When you've failed to get a refill
When you're still hanging around
As you begin to trickle down
Keep a stiff upper lip.
If you're jaywalking in hell
If you're trespassing in paradise
When you're breaking out of purgatory
When reincarnation is overdo

And your re-invented self isn't you
Keep a stiff upper lip.
But not when someone tells you to.

Out of the Box

Relativity
Different references frames
Longer coffee breaks

In Einstein City
Standing on top of large brains
Deluxe apartments

No more politics
Ubiquitous field theory
Genders realign

Storms on Jupiter
Weather for all occasions
New spring arrivals

The sun will go out
Thirty billion years from now
A summer rental

New maps to be drawn
Why be what we resemble
An autumn garden

Time becoming space
Something to look forward to
New container laws

Inside the spaceship
Not much going on out there
Along for the ride

Kryptonite candy
Clark Kent looks for a phone booth
Information please

Igloo News

A beardless eel broke to shattered pedal points.
Quite nice; reminds one of ice.
An icy eel. How does it feel?
More burning than Nod,
Less than a blink
Sliding through the dell of the gnat
A beardless eel below the flow,
Stiffened his glow to dance the life
Of a coruscating glissando.